A Note From Rick Renner

I am on a personal quest to see a "revival of the Bible" so people can establish their lives on a firm foundation that will stand strong and endure the test as end-time storm winds begin to intensify.

In order to experience a revival of the Bible in your personal life, it is important to take time each day to read, receive, and apply its truths to your life. James tells us that if we will continue in the perfect law of liberty — refusing to be forgetful hearers, but determined to be doers — we will be blessed in our ways. As you watch or listen to the programs in this series and work through this corresponding study guide, I trust you will search the Scriptures and allow the Holy Spirit to help you hear something new from God's Word that applies specifically to your life. I encourage you to be a doer of the Word He reveals to you. Whatever the cost, I assure you — it will be worth it.

> Thy words were found, and I did eat them;
> and thy word was unto me the joy and rejoicing of mine heart:
> for I am called by thy name, O Lord God of hosts.
> — Jeremiah 15:16

Your brother and friend in Jesus Christ,

Rick Renner

Victory That Overcomes the World

Copyright © 2025 by Teaching You Can Trust, LLC
1814 W. Tacoma St.
Broken Arrow, OK 74012-1406

Published by Rick Renner Ministries
www.renner.org

ISBN 13: 978-1-6675-1491-8

ISBN 13 eBook: 978-1-6675-1492-5

How To Use This Study Guide

This five-lesson study guide corresponds to *"Victory That Overcomes the World" With Rick Renner* (**Renner TV**). Each lesson in this study guide covers a topic that is addressed during the program series, with questions and references supplied to draw you deeper into your own private study of the Scriptures on this subject.

To derive the most benefit from this study guide, consider the following:

First, watch or listen to the program prior to working through the corresponding lesson in this guide. (Programs can also be viewed at **renner.org** by clicking on the Media/Archives links or on our Renner Ministries YouTube channel.)

Second, take the time to look up the scriptures included in each lesson. Prayerfully consider their application to your own life.

Third, use a journal or notebook to make note of your answers to each lesson's Study Questions and Practical Application challenges.

Fourth, invest specific time in prayer and in the Word of God to consult with the Holy Spirit. Write down the scriptures or insights He reveals to you.

Finally, take action! Whatever the Lord tells you to do according to His Word, do it.

For added insights on this subject, it is recommended that you obtain Rick Renner's book *My Victory-Filled Day — A Sparkling Gems From the Greek Guided Devotional Journal.* You may also select from Rick's other available resources by placing your order at **renner.org** or by calling **1-800-742-5593**.

TOPIC

Victory Is Yours To Claim!

SCRIPTURES

1. **1 John 5:4** — For whatsoever is born of God overcometh the world: and this is the victory that overcometh the world, even our faith.

2. **Luke 11:21-22** — When a strong man armed keepeth his palace, his goods are in peace: but when a stronger than he shall come upon him, and overcome him, he taketh from him all his armour wherein he trusted, and divideth his spoils.

3. **John 16:33** — These things I have spoken unto you, that in me ye might have peace. In the world ye shall have tribulation: but be of good cheer; I have overcome the world.

4. **Romans 3:3-4** — For what if some did not believe? shall their unbelief make the faith of God without effect? God forbid: yea, let God be true, but every man a liar; as it is written, That thou mightest be justified in thy sayings, and mightest overcome when thou art judged.

5. **Romans 12:21** — Be not overcome of evil, but overcome evil with good.

6. **1 John 2:13** — I write unto you, fathers, because ye have known him that is from the beginning. I write unto you, young men, because ye have overcome the wicked one. I write unto you, little children, because ye have known the Father.

7. **1 John 2:14** — I have written unto you, fathers, because ye have known him that is from the beginning. I have written unto you, young men, because ye are strong, and the word of God abideth in you, and ye have overcome the wicked one.

8. **1 John 2:14** *(RIV)* — I have written to you, fathers, because you have really known the One from the beginning of time and even before time as we know it. I have written to you, younger men, because you really are [spiritually] mighty, robust, and strong, and the Word of God steadfastly abides inside you, and you have conquered, mastered, and victoriously overcome the one who is foul, hostile, impure, malicious, malignant, savage, vicious, and vile.

9. **1 John 4:4** — Ye are of God, little children, and have overcome them: because greater is he that is in you, than he that is in the world.

10. **1 John 5:5** — Who is he that overcometh the world, but he that believeth that Jesus is the Son of God?

11. **Revelation 2:7** — He that hath an ear, let him hear what the Spirit saith unto the churches; to him that overcometh will I give to eat of the tree of life, which is in the midst of the paradise of God.

12. **Revelation 2:11** — He that hath an ear, let him hear what the Spirit saith unto the churches; he that overcometh shall not be hurt of the second death.

13. **Revelation 2:17** — He that hath an ear, let him hear what the Spirit saith unto the churches; to him that overcometh will I give to eat of the hidden manna, and will give him a white stone, and in the stone a new name written, which no man knoweth saving he that receiveth it.

14. **Revelation 2:26** — And he that overcometh, and keepeth my works unto the end, to him will I give power over the nations.

15. **Revelation 3:5** — He that overcometh, the same shall be clothed in white raiment; and I will not blot out his name out of the book of life, but I will confess his name before my Father, and before his angels.

16. **Revelation 3:12** — Him that overcometh will I make a pillar in the temple of my God, and he shall go no more out: and I will write upon him the name of my God, and the name of the city of my God, which is new Jerusalem, which cometh down out of heaven from my God: and I will write upon him my new name.

17. **Revelation 3:21** (*NKJV*) — To him who overcomes I will grant to sit with Me on My throne, as I also overcame and sat down with My Father on His throne.

18. **Revelation 5:5** — And one of the elders saith unto me, Weep not: behold, the Lion of the tribe of Judah, the Root of David, hath prevailed to open the book, and to loose the seven seals thereof.

19. **Revelation 6:2** — And I saw, and behold a white horse: and he that sat on him had a bow; and a crown was given unto him: and he went forth conquering, and to conquer.

20. **Revelation 11:7** — And when they shall have finished their testimony, the beast that ascendeth out of the bottomless pit shall make war against them, and shall overcome them, and kill them.

21. **Revelation 12:11** — And they overcame him by the blood of the Lamb, and by the word of their testimony; and they loved not their lives unto the death.

22. **Revelation 13:7** — And it was given unto him to make war with the saints, and to overcome them: and power was given him over all kindreds, and tongues, and nations.

23. **Revelation 15:2** — And I saw as it were a sea of glass mingled with fire: and them that had gotten the victory over the beast, and over his image, and over his mark, and over the number of his name, stand on the sea of glass, having the harps of God.

24. **Revelation 17:14** — These shall make war with the Lamb, and the Lamb shall overcome them: for he is Lord of lords, and King of kings: and they that are with him are called, and chosen, and faithful.

25. **Revelation 21:7** — He that overcometh shall inherit all things; and I will be his God, and he shall be my son.

26. **1 John 5:4** (*RIV*) — For whoever has been born from God conquers, defeats, prevails, and victoriously overcomes the world and all that is in it: and this is the overcoming victory that overcomes and overrides the world and all that is in it, even our faith.

GREEK WORDS

1. "overcometh" or "victory" — **νικάω** (*nikao*) or **νίκη** (*nike*): one who is overcoming; a champion, victor, or one who possesses some type of superiority; it can be translated to control, to conquer, to defeat, to master, to overcome, to overwhelm, to surpass, or to be victorious; used in Greek literature to portray athletes who had mastered their sport and ultimately reigned supreme as champions in the games; it could also describe a military victory of one foe against the other; it means to be permanently and consistently undeterred in one's efforts to overcome and to obtain a lasting victory

2. "born" — **γεγεννημένον** (*gegennemenon*): having been born

3. "of God" — **ἐκ τοῦ Θεοῦ** (*ek tou Theou*): the word **ἐκ** (*ek*) means out, as out of or out from, and **τοῦ Θεοῦ** (*tou Theou*) means of God

4. "the world" — **τὸν κόσμον** (*ton kosmon*): a definite article with the word **κόσμος** (*kosmos*); used to describe everything in the world around us

SYNOPSIS

The five lessons in this study on *Victory That Overcomes the World* will focus on the following topics:

- Victory Is Yours To Claim!
- What Was Jesus' Greatest Triumph?
- Can You Overcome the World?
- How Did Jesus Describe Overcoming?
- Can You Access Overcoming Power?

The emphasis of this lesson:

God has called *you* to be an overcomer in this life — and the Bible makes this abundantly clear! When you are born again, you receive power in your inner man to master the world and all that's in it. Like an Olympic champion who reigns supreme in athletic games, your faith in Christ empowers you to remain undeterred as you press forward and obtain lasting victory over your circumstances.

Do You Know What the Bible Says About You?

As a child of God, you have a faith that overcomes the world. You are called to be victorious. Listen to what the Bible says about you in First John 5:4, which begins by declaring, "For whatsoever is born of God...." Have you been born of God? If you have, you can put your name in this verse. It's describing you! The full verse exhorts, "For whatsoever is born of God overcometh the world: and this is the victory that overcometh the world, even our faith."

Notice that this verse contains the word "overcometh" twice, as well as the word "victory." In the original Greek language, these are different forms of the same word — *nikao* and *nike* — appearing three times in this verse. Furthermore, these same words "overcometh" and "victory" appear 28 times in the New Testament. In this lesson, we'll take a deep dive throughout the entire New Testament so you can see every place where these words are used.

The Greek words for "overcometh" and "victory" depict *one who is overcoming or is in the process of overcoming*. Both words denote *a champion, a victor*, or *one who possesses some kind of superiority*. In Greek literature, they were used to portray *athletes who mastered their sport and ultimately reigned supreme as champions in the games.* The words *nikao* and *nike* could also describe *a military victory of one foe against another.* These Greek words mean *to be permanently and consistently undeterred in one's efforts to overcome and to obtain a lasting victory.*

The words *nikao* and *nike* do not describe a temporary victory, but rather *a lasting victory.* They can be translated *to control, to conquer, to defeat, to master, to overcome, to overwhelm, to surpass,* or *to be victorious.* All these ideas are contained in the words "overcometh" and "victory." God has called *you* to be an overcomer — that's who you are.

When First John 5:4 declares that "whatsoever is born of God" overcomes the world, it's quite a statement. It means you are called to control your environment — you're called to conquer and master the world. You're divinely appointed to overcome it, overwhelm it, and surpass it. You are to be victorious over the world and everything in the world system. And according to this verse, you do it with your faith.

Called To Be Overcomers in *This* World

Now let's examine every use of the words "overcome" and "victory" in the New Testament. In Luke 11:21-22, Jesus declares, "When a strong man armed keepeth his palace, his goods are in peace: but when a stronger than he shall come upon him, and overcome him…." Here we have a form of this Greek word *nikao* or *nike,* meaning *one who overcomes, one who prevails,* or *one who conquers.* The word "overcome" describes one who is *a mighty, mighty overcomer.*

Next we come to John 16:33, in which Jesus declares, "These things I have spoken unto you, that in me ye might have peace. In the world ye shall have tribulation: but be of good cheer; I have overcome the world." When Jesus proclaims, "Be of good cheer," the original Greek text could be rendered, "Speak to yourself and cheer yourself up because I have prevailed over the world. I've overcome and maintained victory over the world." All this is found in this word "overcome."

Romans 3:3 and 4 instructs us, "For what if some did not believe? shall their unbelief make the faith of God without effect? God forbid: yea, let God be true, but every man a liar; as it is written, That thou mightest be justified in thy sayings, and mightest overcome when thou art judged."

Here we have a picture of one who is overcoming. The word "overcome" is simply so powerful!

We have such good counsel from the Holy Spirit in Romans 12:21: "Be not overcome of evil, but overcome evil with good." This verse tells us not to be conquered or controlled by evil but rather to surpass evil. Conquer evil with good. Again, we are called to be overcomers.

It's a Done Deal — You *Have* Overcome

First John 2:13 states, "I write unto you, fathers, because ye have known him that is from the beginning. I write unto you, young men, because ye have overcome the wicked one. I write unto you, little children, because ye have known the Father." Again, we see God has called us to overcome.

Verse 14 continues, "I have written unto you, fathers, because ye have known him that is from the beginning. I have written unto you, young men, because ye are strong, and the word of God abideth in you, and ye have overcome the wicked one." Once again, we find the word "overcome." Factoring in the original Greek meaning of this passage, the *Renner Interpretive Version* (*RIV*) of First John 2:14 says:

> **I have written to you, fathers, because you have really known the One from the beginning of time and even before time as we know it. I have written to you, younger men, because you really are [spiritually] mighty, robust, and strong, and the Word of God steadfastly abides inside you, and you have conquered, mastered, and victoriously overcome the one who is foul, hostile, impure, malicious, malignant, savage, vicious, and vile.**

Take note of the phrase "you have conquered, mastered, and victoriously overcome." This is a translation of the Greek word *nikao*, which depicts us as *overcomers*. Next let's look at First John 4:4, which declares, "Ye are of God, little children, and have overcome them: because greater is he that is in you, than he that is in the world." Notice the phrase "have overcome" is past tense — it's a done deal. You have overcome because greater is He that is in you than he that is in the world.

Let's look again at First John 5:4, which states, "For whatsoever is born of God overcometh the world: and this is the victory that overcometh the world, even our faith." In this one verse, some form of the Greek words *nikao* and *nike* are repeated three times as "overcometh" and "victory."

First John 5:5 goes on to observe, "Who is he that overcometh the world, but he that believeth that Jesus is the Son of God?" This verse means everyone who is born again and believes Jesus is the Son of God is called to be an overcomer in life. Victory is yours to claim!

Jesus Invites You To Be an Overcomer

Now we come to Revelation 2:7, which states, "He that hath an ear, let him hear what the Spirit saith unto the churches; to him that overcometh will I give to eat of the tree of life, which is in the midst of the paradise of God." Jesus invites all believers to be overcomers. That's God's call for you: You are to be victorious.

God has called you to conquer and master the world and everything in it! This includes your health and finances, as well as troubles and strife. God has given you the power to override and overcome it all. Look at what else Revelation has to say about this invitation from Jesus to be an overcomer:

He that hath an ear, let him hear what the Spirit saith unto the churches; he that overcometh shall not be hurt of the second death.
— Revelation 2:11

He that hath an ear, let him hear what the Spirit saith unto the churches; to him that overcometh will I give to eat of the hidden manna, and will give him a white stone, and in the stone a new name written, which no man knoweth saving he that receiveth it.
— Revelation 2:17

And he that overcometh, and keepeth my works unto the end, to him will I give power over the nations.
— Revelation 2:26

He that overcometh, the same shall be clothed in white raiment; and I will not blot out his name out of the book of life, but I will confess his name before my Father, and before his angels.
— Revelation 3:5

Him that overcometh will I make a pillar in the temple of my God, and he shall go no more out: and I will write upon him the name of my God, and the name of the city of my God, which

is new Jerusalem, which cometh down out of heaven from my
God: and I will write upon him my new name.

— Revelation 3:12

To him who overcomes I will grant to sit with Me on My
throne, as I also overcame and sat down with My Father on His
throne.

— Revelation 3:21 (*NKJV*)

Jesus is an overcomer, and He challenges us to be overcomers. Friend, you
are not to be a victim. You are not to throw in the towel. You are called
to be a prevailing force. God wants you to be an overcomer, not one who
easily gives up. He has called you to triumph in life.

You Are Made To Prevail

In Revelation 5:5, we read, "And one of the elders saith unto me, Weep not:
behold, the Lion of the tribe of Judah, the Root of David, hath prevailed to
open the book, and to loose the seven seals thereof." The word "prevailed" in
this verse is the same root word that is translated elsewhere as "overcome."
In the original Greek, it is the word for "victory," meaning *to have a victorious position.*

We see this same concept in Revelation 6:2, which says, "And I saw, and
behold a white horse: and he that sat on him had a bow; and a crown was
given unto him: and he went forth conquering, and to conquer." In the
original Greek language of this verse, the word translated here as "conquering" and "conquer" means *to prevail* or *to have victory.*

Revelation 11:7 says, "And when they shall have finished their testimony,
the beast that ascendeth out of the bottomless pit shall make war against
them, and shall overcome them, and kill them." In this verse, we find
another version of this same word that means *a mighty, prevailing force.*

This idea of prevailing also comes forth in Revelation 12:11, which
declares, "And they overcame him by the blood of the Lamb, and by the
word of their testimony; and they loved not their lives unto the death."
The word "overcame" in this verse is also a form of the Greek word *nikao.*
It describes believers as *prevailing, conquering, and overcoming even in the
worst of times.*

Victory Belongs to God and His People

Continuing on our study of the word "overcome," let's look at Revelation 13:7, which says, "And it was given unto him to make war with the saints, and to overcome them: and power was given him over all kindreds, and tongues, and nations." This verse highlights an event that will take place during the Great Tribulation. For a limited period of time, the Antichrist will be given power to overcome and to conquer the world.

Revelation 15:2 says, "And I saw as it were a sea of glass mingled with fire: and them that had gotten the victory over the beast, and over his image, and over his mark, and over the number of his name, stand on the sea of glass, having the harps of God." The word "victory" here is the same Greek word *nikao* that we have been studying in this lesson. It means they *prevailed, conquered*, and *gained victory* over the beast.

Revelation 17:14 continues this theme, revealing, "These shall make war with the Lamb, and the Lamb shall overcome them: for he is Lord of lords, and King of kings: and they that are with him are called, and chosen, and faithful." Again, "overcome" is a form of *nikao*, which depicts *a prevailing, mighty force.*

And finally, Revelation 21:7 declares, "He that overcometh shall inherit all things; and I will be his God, and he shall be my son." God has called you to be an overcomer, and now you have seen every instance — all 28 — of the words "overcome" and "victory" used in the pages of the New Testament.

You Can Triumph Over the World and All That's in It

Let's take another look at First John 4:4 — "Ye are of God, little children, and have overcome them: because greater is he that is in you, than he that is in the world." This verse reminds us that our victory begins with God's presence within us. The power of the Holy Spirit within us is greater than the force or influence of anyone who lives in the world. Because of that indwelling power, we are already positioned as overcomers.

Now looking again at First John 5:4, we read, "For whatsoever is born of God overcometh the world: and this is the victory that overcometh the world, even our faith." The phrase "whatsoever is born of God" really means *whoever* is born of God — if you've accepted Christ, then that includes you! This verse promises and guarantees that whatever or whoever is born of God "overcometh the world." In the Greek language, the word "overcometh" is in the present tense, indicating continuous action. It means that *right now*, in this very moment, you are overcoming the world.

The expression "the world" is the Greek phrase *ton kosmon*, which describes *the world and everything in the world.* This verse means you have an overcoming ability to triumph over the world, the world system, and every single thing that will ever try to come against you. This is the victory that overcomes the world and everything in it — even our faith.

Victory Is Yours To Claim *Today*

The word "overcometh" repeatedly describes one who is overcoming, one who is constantly championing, being victorious, and possessing superiority. That's who God has called you to be! You are called *to conquer, to defeat, to master, to overcome, to overwhelm, to surpass*, or *to be victorious.* As mentioned earlier in this lesson, the term *nikao* or *nike* was used in Greek literature to portray *athletes who mastered their sports and reigned supreme as champions in the games.* It could be used militarily to describe *the victory of one foe against another*, and it means *to be permanently and consistently undeterred in one's efforts to overcome and to obtain a lasting victory.*

It is important to understand how the words "overcometh" and "victory" are used in the New Testament. When the Bible says whatsoever is born of God overcomes the world, it's talking about *you.* God has called *you* to be a prevailing force and to overcome absolutely everything in the world around you. Friend, you're *called* to be an overcomer. You *are* an overcomer. And you *will be* an overcomer because greater is He that is in you than he that is in the world (*see* 1 John 4:4). Jesus has called you to have victory in your life, and *victory is yours to claim.*

What are you surrounded with today that you need to overcome? Whatever you may face, you can overcome it because the Greater One lives in you. Embrace the one who is in you, release the power of God, and rise up to be the overcomer He has called you to be.

STUDY QUESTIONS

Study to shew thyself approved unto God, a workman that needeth
not to be ashamed, rightly dividing the word of truth.
— 2 Timothy 2:15

1. First John 4:4 says, "Ye are of God, little children, and have overcome
   them: because greater is he that is in you, than he that is in the world."
   Think about it! You *have* overcome — it's a done deal! What tense is
   used in the following passages? How does that ignite your faith for
   victory?

   - **1 John 2:13** — "...I write unto you, young men, because ye *have*
     overcome the wicked one...."

   - **1 John 2:14** — "...I have written unto you, young men, because ye
     are strong, and the word of God abideth in you, and ye *have over-*
     come the wicked one."

2. Is overcoming automatic, or do you have a part to play? What does
   First Peter 5:8 tell us about the importance of vigilance as part of an
   overcomer's life?

3. You can "reign in life by one, Jesus Christ" (*see* Romans 5:17). Your
   triumph over whatever you're facing is certain because of Jesus' victory. What else does the Bible tell us about winning life's challenges
   through Christ?

   - "...We are more than conquerors *through him* that loved us"
     (Romans 8:37).

   - "But thanks be to God, which giveth us the victory *through our Lord*
     Jesus Christ" (1 Corinthians 15:57).

   - "I can do all things *through Christ* which strengtheneth me"
     (Philippians 4:13).

PRACTICAL APPLICATION

But be ye doers of the word, and not hearers only,
deceiving your own selves.
— James 1:22

1. The words "overcometh" and "victory" are used 28 times in the New
   Testament. In this lesson, Rick took a deep dive into what it means to

be an overcomer. Which verse from this lesson stood out most to you? What are some practical ways you can be a "doer" of these verses?

2. In light of the Word of God that clearly states you are an overcomer, take inventory of your thought life. Do you *think* like a champion, a victor, and one who conquers, defeats, masters, and overcomes? Do you *think* like one who reigns supreme as a *champion* in life? Jesus paid the price for you to live victoriously now and in the future. In what areas of your life do you think like an overcomer — and in what areas do you need to improve?

3. When the Bible says whatever is born of God overcomes the world, it's talking about *you*! God has called *you* to be a prevailing force and to overcome absolutely everything in the world around you. Think about it: You're *called* — by God — to be an overcomer. You *are* an overcomer. And you *will be* an overcomer because greater is He that is in you than he that is in the world. Take time to meditate on this amazing truth and write out any insights the Holy Spirit highlights to you.

LESSON 2

TOPIC
What Was Jesus' Greatest Triumph?

SCRIPTURES

1. **Colossians 2:15** — And having spoiled principalities and powers, he made a shew of them openly, triumphing over them in it.

2. **2 Corinthians 2:14** — Now thanks be unto God, which always causeth us to triumph in Christ, and maketh manifest the savour of his knowledge by us in every place.

GREEK WORDS

1. "spoiled" — ἀπεκδύομαι (*apekduomai*): to put off; to strip off, as one would strip off garments; used to depict the disarming of an enemy; to strip an enemy of his weaponry and artillery and leave him without any weapons with which to respond; to strip an enemy to the point of complete nakedness; to thoroughly plunder

2. "principalities" — τὰς ἀρχὰς (*tas archas*): plural, meaning the princi-palities; used to refer to all high-ranking beings of a spiritual nature, but specifically here it refers to dark forces

3. "powers" — τὰς ἐξουσίας (*tas exousias*): plural, referring to those who have received authority to exercise influence, particularly a dark type of spiritual influence

4. "shew" — δειγματίζω (*deigmatidzo*): to display or to expose some-thing; used to denote the display of captives, weaponry, and trophies that were seized during war on foreign soil; once the war was finished and the battle was won, the reigning emperor would return home and victoriously display and expose the treasures, trophies, weaponry, and captives that he had seized during his military conquest; this was a grand moment of celebration for the victor, but a humiliating experi-ence for the defunct foe

5. "openly" — ἐν παρρησίᾳ (*en parresia*): in the wide open, hence, for all to see; publicly

6. "triumphing" — θριαμβεύω (*thriambeuo*): a word used to describe a general or an emperor returning home from a grand victory; it depicts the general or emperor's triumphal parade when he returned home with the beaten foreign ruler bound in chains and forced him to walk behind him in disgrace, shame, dishonor, embarrassment, and humili-ation, as crowds of people celebrated his defeat

SYNOPSIS

The Bible makes clear that after Jesus died on the Cross, He descended into hell. During His three days in the grave, He plundered the enemy's territory and stripped principalities and powers of all authority. He made an open show of the enemy's complete defeat and returned to Heaven as the ultimate conqueror over hell and death — and He shares this victory with you! As a born-again believer, the Greater One lives in you, empow-ering you to walk in victory.

The emphasis of this lesson:

Christ has triumphed over all — and He has called and empowered you to triumph too! He has stripped the enemy bare and totally removed all his weapons. Now, the devil is powerless over Christ, and he is power-less over you too. The Greater One lives in you, and you have the ability to always triumph in Christ!

United by One Faith, One Creed

At Moscow Good News Church, which Rick and Denise founded and pastored for many years, the church members quote the Apostles' Creed every single week without fail. Some might say, "Why do they do that? This seems very religious." They do it because the people who attend the church have come from many different backgrounds. Some have come from other denominations, while others were once atheists. So when they come to church, Pastor Paul Renner wants to make sure everyone is on the same page about what they believe.

The Apostles' Creed is one of the oldest creeds of the Church. Here is what it says:

APOSTLES' CREED

I believe in God, the Father Almighty,

the Creator of Heaven and earth,

and in Jesus Christ, His only Son, our Lord:

Who was conceived of the Holy Spirit,

born of the Virgin Mary,

suffered under Pontius Pilate,

was crucified, died, and was buried.

He descended into hell.

The third day He arose again from the dead.

He ascended into Heaven

and sits at the right hand of God the Father Almighty,

whence He shall come to judge the living and the dead.

I believe in the Holy Spirit,

the holy catholic [universal] Church,

the communion of saints,

the forgiveness of sins,

the resurrection of the body,

and life everlasting.

Amen.

The word "catholic" here doesn't refer to the Roman Catholic church. Instead, the word "catholic" means *universal*. In the program, Rick stated that he and Denise, as well as their church, believe every point stated in the Apostles' Creed. RENNER Ministries stands behind each of these core beliefs, as they are the truths that anchor our faith.

Jesus Literally Plundered Hell

There is one statement in the Apostles' Creed that remains debated today, even though it has been part of the Church's oldest and most foundational creed for centuries — the phrase, "He descended into hell."

Today there are many Christians who don't believe Jesus went to hell. They say, "No, He just went to the grave." But the Bible explicitly teaches that in the three days when Jesus' body was in the grave, His spirit descended into hell. In fact, Jesus literally plundered hell at the end of those three days. We see this plainly in the Scriptures.

Colossians 2:15 declares, "And having spoiled principalities and powers, he made a shew of them openly, triumphing over them in it." The *principalities and powers* mentioned here refer to the demonic rulers and spiritual forces that opposed God's plan. Jesus stripped these powers of their authority through His work on the Cross — and He completely defeated them through what He accomplished during those three days when He was in hell.

Jesus Deprived the Enemy of All Power

Let's take apart Colossians 2:15, beginning with the phrase "…having spoiled principalities and powers…." The word "spoiled" in the Greek language is *apekduomai*, which means *to put off or to strip off, as one would strip off garments*. It was a technical word that depicted *the disarming of an enemy*. It means *to disarm an enemy, to strip an enemy of his weaponry and artillery and to leave him absolutely without any weapons with which to respond, to strip him bare, to strip an enemy to the point of complete nakedness*, or *to thoroughly plunder*.

This verse could be better translated like this: "He completely stripped principalities and powers and left them utterly naked, with nothing left at their disposal to retaliate." What a powerful word! For three days, the enemy thought he had won with Jesus in hell. But on the third day, God quickened Jesus by the power of the Holy Spirit. And as Jesus reentered

His body on the way out of hell, He *completely stripped* principalities and powers and *left them utterly naked with nothing left at their disposal with which to retaliate.* He stripped them bare.

Who was it that Jesus stripped bare? The verse tells us it was "principalities and powers." In the original Greek, these terms are plural. The word "principalities" is the Greek phrase *tas archas*, which refers to *all high-ranking beings of a spiritual nature, but specifically to dark spiritual beings and those of the satanic or demonic realm.* The word "powers" is the Greek plural phrase *tas exousias*, which refers to *those who had authority in the dark, demonic realm to exercise influence, particularly a dark type of spiritual influence.*

Jesus literally stripped these principalities and powers bare and "made a shew of them openly." The word "shew" is the Greek word *deigmatidzo*, which conveys the meaning *to display* or *to expose something.* It was used to denote *the display of captives, weaponry, and trophies that were seized during war on foreign soil.* Once the war was finished and the battle was won, the reigning emperor would return home and would victoriously display or expose the treasures, the trophies, the weaponry, and captives that he had seized during his military conquest. This was a grand moment of celebration for the victor, but a humiliating experience for the defunct foe.

This verse tells us explicitly that Jesus stripped principalities and powers naked and left them with nothing with which to retaliate. He stripped them bare to the core as He ascended from hell back into Heaven.

Jesus Made a Glorious Display of His Utter Triumph

Colossians 2:15 goes on to declare that Jesus "…made a shew of them openly, triumphing over them in it." In the Greek, the word "openly" is the phrase *en parresia.* The term *en* means *in,* and the term *parresia* describes *boldness, confidence,* or *something that's very frank.* When compounded with *en,* we get the expression *en parresia,* meaning to do something *in the wide open for all to see very publicly.*

What Jesus did in hell was no quiet affair. In fact, it was quite a public event. He did it openly and loudly. He displayed this now-defunct foe to all of Heaven's host and revealed that He had plundered hell. He stripped bare the enemy and seized all his artillery and weaponry.

The verse goes on to say that when Jesus did this, He was "…triumphing over them in it" (Colossians 2:15). The Greek word for "triumphing" is *thriambeuo*, a very important term used to describe *a general or an emperor returning home from a grand victory*. It depicts *the general or emperor's triumphal parade when he returned home with a beaten foreign ruler bound in chains and forced to walk behind him in disgrace, shame, dishonor, embarrassment, and humiliation*.

When the Romans achieved a great victory, crowds of people would fill the streets and throw a celebration. It was the wildest party of all because the emperor had returned home, and he reigned victorious. Triumphal parades were momentous affairs, and they occurred quite frequently, always after a grand conquest. When the emperor or a great general returned home, he rode in his chariot, which was decked in gold and pulled by magnificent horses.

The emperor or general rode at the very front of the parade. Behind him was the foreign enemy that he had defeated, bound in chains, often in a cage or sometimes forced to walk in humiliation and shame. Then came the defeated foe's generals, his nobles, and all his men of war, who were also walking behind their defunct leader in total shame and humiliation.

Behind this display, there would be carts loaded with treasures, trophies, and all kinds of spoils that the emperor or the general had seized from that foreign territory and was bringing home. This was a moment of great praise and triumph for the emperor or the general because he was reigning. But for the defeated foe, this was the greatest shame and humiliation of all.

The Enemy Has Been Completely Stripped Bare

Maybe you have heard of Cleopatra, known as Cleopatra VII and the queen of Egypt. When Egypt fell in 30 BC, she knew she would be treated as a defeated foe. Caesar (Augustus) would take her to Rome, where she would be put on public display in chains or perhaps in a cage. She knew that behind her would be her son and other Egyptian rulers and nobles who were now defeated, and behind them the treasures of Egypt would be put on display as spoils.

The streets were going to be filled with Roman citizens who came together to celebrate the returning emperor and see the defeated Cleopatra. Rather than face the shame of that moment, she chose to commit suicide. She did not want to be put on display.

With all this in mind, let's look at Colossians 2:15 one more time, which says, "And having spoiled principalities and powers, he made a shew of them openly, triumphing over them in it." The word "spoiled" means Jesus *completely stripped principalities and powers and left them utterly naked with nothing left at their disposal to retaliate.* And he did this *openly* — in the wide open for all the heavenly realm, every spiritual realm, to see. Figuratively, the apostle Paul declared that when Jesus returned home after this event and ascended to Heaven, He returned as the reigning emperor. Heaven threw a party!

Jesus had been to the depths of the depths. He had spent three days in the enemy's camp. The enemy thought he had defeated Jesus. But on the third day, God said, in essence, "I will not allow My Holy One to suffer corruption" (*see* Psalm 16:10; Acts 2:27). The power of the Holy Spirit descended into the very pit of hell itself and divinely energized Jesus. And on the way out, Jesus stripped the enemy bare. Christ triumphed over the enemy. He led a triumphal procession and displayed this now-defunct devil as completely, utterly humiliated and stripped bare of all his weaponry. This is just so powerful!

God *Always* Causes You To Triumph — *Always*!

But wait — there's something else! Second Corinthians 2:14 exhorts, "Now thanks be unto God, which always causeth us to triumph in Christ, and maketh manifest the savour of his knowledge by us in every place." Just as Jesus jubilantly triumphed over the enemy, this verse declares that God *always* causes *us* to triumph.

Victory is yours to claim. God has called you to be an overcomer. He has called you to be a victor, not a victim — one who overcomes everything that is around you. In the same way that Christ triumphed, Second Corinthians 2:14 says God "...always causeth us to triumph in Christ...."

Friend, if you're not triumphing over everything in your life right now, then you've not hit the mark yet, because God always causes us to triumph over *everything*. He empowers you to triumph over strife, over the enemy, over sickness, over failure, and even over a bad self-image. God has called you to triumph over it all and put the enemy on display. The enemy has been stripped naked, and he is under your feet!

STUDY QUESTIONS

Study to shew thyself approved unto God, a workman that needeth
not to be ashamed, rightly dividing the word of truth.
— 2 Timothy 2:15

1. When Jesus' body was in the grave for three days, His spirit went to
    hell — but He didn't stay there! By the power of the Holy Spirit, He
    stripped the enemy bare and triumphed over the devil. Jesus led a
    triumphal procession and displayed the defeated enemy as completely,
    utterly humiliated and stripped bare of all his weaponry. Jesus went to
    hell in our place and overcame the evil one. What else did Jesus do in
    our place? (*Consider* Isaiah 53:4-5; 2 Corinthians 8:9; and 1 Peter 2:24.)

2. Read Ephesians 2:5 and 6, which says, "Even when we were dead in
    sins, hath quickened us together with Christ, (by grace ye are saved;)
    and hath raised us up together, and made us sit together in heavenly
    places in Christ Jesus." When God quickened Jesus (the head), He
    quickened the Body of Christ. When God raised Jesus, He raised the
    Body. According to these verses, where are you seated *in Christ*?

3. Ephesians 1:19-23 declares the exceeding greatness of God's power,
    demonstrated when He raised Christ from the dead and placed Him
    at His right hand, far above all powers and authorities. Because all
    things are under Christ's authority and you are in Him, what does this
    passage teach you about the authority and victory you have in your
    own life?

PRACTICAL APPLICATION

But be ye doers of the word, and not hearers only,
deceiving your own selves.
— James 1:22

1. You have authority! You are called to have victory, to overcome, and
    to triumph. You're meant to walk in victory — not just sometimes,
    but *always*. God *always* causes you to triumph in Christ. Are there
    areas in your life where you have not been walking in victory? How
    can you begin to embrace the truth that God has called you to always
    triumph? Write down or declare aloud: "I always triumph in Christ!"
    Then take a moment and identify one practical step you can take this
    week to live in that victory.

2. Greater is He that is in you, which means you can overcome every-
    thing in Jesus' name. Take a moment and identify one challenge you
    are facing — it could be sickness, stress, financial difficulty, or conflict.
    Meditate on Second Corinthians 2:14, and by faith, thank God for
    your victory.

3. Jesus plundered hell. He stripped the enemy bare to the core as He
    ascended from hell back into Heaven. Jesus' triumph over hell is not just
    historical — it affects how you live today. How can this truth change
    the way you face fear, opposition, or discouragement in your daily life?
    Name one specific way you will intentionally remind yourself of Christ's
    victory this week (for example, through prayer, worship, Scripture mem-
    ory, or bold action in faith).

TOPIC

Can You Overcome the World?

SCRIPTURES

1. **John 16:33** — These things I have spoken unto you, that in me ye
    might have peace. In the world ye shall have tribulation: but be of
    good cheer; I have overcome the world.

2. **2 Corinthians 1:8** — For we would not, brethren, have you ignorant
    of our trouble which came to us in Asia, that we were pressed out of
    measure, above strength, insomuch that we despaired even of life.

3. **2 Corinthians 1:9** — But we had the sentence of death in ourselves,
    that we should not trust in ourselves, but in God which raiseth the
    dead.

4. **2 Corinthians 1:8-9** (*RIV*) — We would not, brethren, have you
    ignorant of the horribly tight, life-threatening squeeze that came to us
    in Asia. It was unbelievable! With all the things we've been through,
    this was the worst of all — it felt like our lives were being crushed. It
    was so difficult that I didn't know what to do. No experience I've ever
    been through required so much of me. In fact, I didn't have enough
    strength to cope with it. Toward the end of this ordeal, I was so
    weighed down and overwhelmed that I didn't think we'd ever get out!

I felt suffocated, trapped, and pinned against the wall. I really thought it was the end of the road for us! As far as we were concerned, the verdict was in, and that verdict said "death." But really, this was no great shock, because we already were feeling the effect of death and depression in our souls.

5. **2 Corinthians 1:10** — Who delivered us from so great a death, and doth deliver: in whom we trust that he will yet deliver us.

6. **2 Corinthians 1:10** (*RIV*) — Who has already delivered and rescued us from a serious death sentence, and will deliver and rescue us, and we trust he will keep on delivering and rescuing us.

GREEK WORDS

1. "tribulation" — θλῖψις (*thlipsis*): used to convey the idea of a heavy-pressure situation; depicts a person who is in a tight place, under a heavy burden, and in a great squeeze

2. "overcome" — νικάω (*nikao*): one who has become a champion, victor, or who possesses some type of superiority; one who has conquered, defeated, mastered, overcome, overwhelmed, surpassed, or who has obtained victory; used in Greek literature to portray athletes who had mastered their sport and ultimately reigned supreme as champions in the games; it could also describe a military victory of one foe against the other; it means to be permanently and consistently undeterred in one's efforts to overcome and to obtain a lasting victory

3. "the world" — τὸν κόσμον (*ton kosmon*): a definite article with the word κόσμος (*kosmos*); used to describe everything in the world around us

4. "ignorant" — ἀγνοέω (*agnoeo*): ignorant or uninformed

5. "trouble" — θλῖψις (*thlipsis*): used to convey the idea of a heavy-pressure situation; depicts a person who is in a tight place, under a heavy burden, and in a great squeeze

6. "pressed out of measure" — καθ' ὑπερβολὴν (*kath huperbolen*): to throw something beyond; describes something that is excessive or beyond the normal range that most people experience

7. "above" — ὑπέρ (*huper*): conveys the idea of something excessive

8. "strength" — δύναμις (*dunamis*): normally indicates phenomenal power and strength

9. "we were weighed down" (*not in the KJV*) — βαρέω (*bareo*): to be heavily weighed down

10. "despaired" — ἐξαπορέω (*exaporeo*): used to describe a situation with no way out; where we get the word exasperated; used to describe individuals who were caught, pinned down, trapped, up against a wall, and utterly hopeless; in today's language, one might say, "Well, sorry, but it looks like this is the end of the road for you!"

11. "sentence" — ἀπόκριμα (*apokrima*): this sentence speaks of a final verdict

12. "delivered" — ῥύομαι (*rhuomai*): has [past tense] delivered us; to deliver or rescue from a dangerous situation; used to depict God delivering and rescuing His people from peril

13. "so great" — τηλικοῦτος (*telikoutos*): enormous, great, or mighty

14. "doth deliver" — ῥύομαι (*rhuomai*): will [future tense] deliver us; to deliver or rescue from a dangerous situation; used to depict God delivering and rescuing His people from peril

15. "yet deliver" — ἔτι ῥύσεται (*eti rhusetai*): will [still or even more] deliver us; to deliver or rescue from a dangerous situation; used to depict God delivering and rescuing His people from peril

SYNOPSIS

Life brings trials, and Jesus did not hide that truth from us. In John 16:33 (*NKJV*), He said plainly, "…In the world you will have tribulation…." Yet Jesus immediately added, "…Be of good cheer; I have overcome the world." Hardships come to us all, bringing moments when life feels unbearably heavy, but we are overcomers in Christ! Just as the apostle Paul faced and overcame tremendous difficulties, you also can overcome — because Jesus shares His amazing victory over the world with you. No matter how hopeless your situation feels, you can rejoice because your Deliverer is faithful, and victory is certain.

The emphasis of this lesson:

God wants every day of your life to be filled with victory, and it is — because Jesus has already overcome the world, and *His* victory guarantees *yours*! Remember, God's deliverance is ongoing. He *has* delivered you, He *is* delivering you, and He *will* deliver you. No burden is too heavy, no trial too overwhelming for His power to overcome in *your* life.

Realize That Trials Come to Us All

You have a victory that overcomes the world! John 16:33 says, "These things I have spoken unto you, that in me ye might have peace. In the world ye shall have tribulation: but be of good cheer; I have overcome the world." Jesus was so honest with us. The fact is, tribulation comes in life. It may be self-inflicted. It may be due to finances or what somebody else has done. It may be a demonic attack. Yes, in life we often hit rough spots, as John 16:33 describes.

This word "tribulation" in this verse is the Greek word *thlipsis*, which the apostle Paul used often in his writings to describe the events that he had been through. It is used to convey the idea of *a heavy-pressure situation*. It depicts *a person who's in a tight place, under a heavy burden, and in a great squeeze*.

This word was first used to denote a type of torture and depicted a man who was laid flat on his back with a big boulder placed over him. The boulder was dropped lower and lower until finally the man felt the full weight of the boulder pressing against him. Those who were in charge would say to the man, "If you don't confess your crime or recant your faith, we'll cut this rope and completely squash you."

If the prisoner refused to comply, his captors would lower the boulder a little bit more until finally he felt the full weight, the *tribulation*, of that boulder pressing down against him. They would tell him again, "Confess your crime or recant your faith." If he refused, they would continue lowering the boulder until finally he was in such a tight squeeze that he could hardly breathe. He felt pinned against the floor, unable to breathe. All of this is contained in the word "tribulation."

Be Encouraged — Jesus Has Overcome the Enemy

When Jesus says, "In this world you will have tribulation," it means that you will come to moments in life when you're in a squeeze or a tight place. Sometimes you'll feel like you can hardly breathe because you're so trapped and pinned by your situation. We can appreciate the fact that the Lord warned us about this. He didn't tell us everything would be rosy and there would never be problems. He said, "In the world, you're going to come to hard spots in life."

But then He said, "But be of good cheer. I have overcome the world." The Greek text here actually says, "Cheer yourself up." This is helpful because there are moments when you have to speak to yourself. Maybe no one else is available to encourage you. In moments like that, you must speak to yourself. You are your greatest preacher. You have a mouth, and you can declare the truth to yourself. There are times when you must do so! Remember all the good that God has done for you. Call those things to remembrance because you may not be remembering the good things.

Jesus said, "Be of good cheer [cheer yourself up]; I have overcome the world." The Greek word for "overcome" is *nikao*. "I have overcome" is present tense — it's a done deal. This term depicts *one who has become a champion, a victor, one who possesses some type of superiority*, or *one who has conquered, defeated, mastered, overcome, overwhelmed, surpassed, or who has obtained victory*. This term was used in Greek literature to portray *athletes who have mastered their sport and reigned supreme as champions in the games*. And it also describes *a military victory over one against another foe*, as well as *to be permanently and consistently undeterred in one's efforts to overcome and obtain a lasting victory*. It means *to control, conquer, defeat, master, overcome, overwhelm, surpass, or be victorious*.

Further, Jesus declared in John 16:33, "…I have overcome the world." In the original Greek, "the world" is the phrase *ton kosmon*, and it means *the world and everything related to it*. There is not one thing in the world that Jesus did not overcome. He overcame death, sickness, and demonic powers. He overcame hell. Jesus has overcome *everything*. If we find ourselves feeling trapped, against the wall, pinned down, and we don't know how to get out of a place of tribulation, that's a moment for us to speak to ourselves. It's a time to cheer ourselves up because Jesus has overcome everything, and He gives to us overcoming power.

God's Delivering Power Is Here for You

In Second Corinthians 1:8-10, the apostle Paul gave an amazing testimony of how he overcame a truly rough spot. He begins by saying, "For we would not, brethren, have you ignorant of our trouble…." The word "trouble" is the same Greek word *thlipsis* that is translated as "tribulation" in John 16:33. In its entirety, Second Corinthians 1:8-10 declares:

> **For we would not, brethren, have you ignorant of our trouble**
> **which came to us in Asia, that we were pressed out of measure,**

above strength, insomuch that we despaired even of life: but we had the sentence of death in ourselves, that we should not trust in ourselves, but in God which raiseth the dead: who delivered us from so great a death, and doth deliver: in whom we trust that he will yet deliver us.

When Paul was ministering in Asia, he encountered an event so intense that it appeared as if he would never escape. But he did escape! God delivered him. And God will deliver you. Jesus has overcome everything. He is the Greater One, and He lives in you (*see* 1 John 4:4). No matter what comes against you, if you'll speak to yourself, cheer yourself up, and grab hold of the power of God, you can overcome anything. That's what we see in this passage.

To fully understand what this passage is saying, let's take these verses apart. First of all, Paul wrote in verse 8, "For we would not, brethren, have you ignorant...." The word "ignorant" is the Greek word *agnoeo*, which describes *one who is uninformed or ignorant*. This verse literally means, "Hey, brethren, we want you to really understand. We don't want you to be unknowledgeable about what we have been through." Paul didn't hide the fact that he went through hard times. In fact, he spoke about his hard times because he wanted to demonstrate that if he could get through what he had been through, anybody can get through what he or she is going through.

Paul went on to state, "For we would not, brethren, have you ignorant of our trouble which came to us in Asia...." The word "trouble" in the Greek is *thlipsis*, the same word translated "tribulation" in John 16:33. Again, it originally described a man lying on the floor with a huge stone pressed against him. The stone would be lowered until finally he couldn't move. He felt pinned, trapped, like he could suffocate. If he wouldn't comply with the request of his torturers, they would cut the stone loose, and he would be completely smashed.

Don't Give Up — No Matter What You Face

Paul went on in Second Corinthians 1:8 to explain, "...We were pressed out of measure, above strength, insomuch that we despaired even of life." In Greek, the phrase "pressed out of measure" is *kath huperbolen*, which means *to throw something beyond*. It describes *something that is excessive or beyond the normal range that most people experience*. It's the equivalent of saying, "What we have been through is beyond anything we have ever previously experienced. It was excessive."

Next, Paul used the phrase "above strength." The term "above" in the original Greek is *huper*, which again conveys the idea of *something that is excessive*. Paul was compounding one term on top of another to describe what he had been through. The Greek word for "strength" here is *dunamis*, which normally indicates *phenomenal power and strength*. But in this verse, it means that what Paul went through was *beyond any strength that he had to endure*.

In the Greek text, there is one more word in this verse that is not found in the King James Version of this verse — the word *bareo*, which means *to be heavily, heavily weighed down*. It describes the very depths of the sea, something very deep and very heavy to carry. Paul was saying that this situation was so heavy, it was weighing him down into the very depths, so that he even despaired of life. Some might say this doesn't sound like a statement of faith, but it is — because Paul didn't give up and he didn't break!

"Despaired" is the Greek word *exaporeo*, and it's where we get the word exasperated. It was used to describe a situation when a person feels he or she has *no way out*. It depicts *an individual who is caught, trapped, up against a wall, or pinned to the floor and feels utterly hopeless*. In today's language, we would say, "It looks like this is the end of the road for me. I'm exasperated. There's no way out of this event that I'm facing." This is what the word "despaired" means in the Greek text.

In Second Corinthians 1:9, Paul explained how deep his despair was when he stated, "But we had the sentence of death in ourselves...." In the Greek text, this phrase "the sentence of death" is the compound word *apokrima* — the word *krima* describes *the verdict of a court*, and when *apo* is added, the resulting term means *a verdict has been handed down*. So Paul was saying that it looked like the verdict of death had been passed upon him. Here, "death" is the Greek word *thanatos*, which describes *a death verdict*.

Our Deliverance Is Past, Present, and Future

What did Paul do when he faced such a terrible situation? The answer is so powerful! Factoring in the original Greek meaning of this passage, the *Renner Interpretive Version* of Second Corinthians 1:8 and 9 says:

We would not, brethren, have you ignorant of the horribly tight, life-threatening squeeze that came to us in Asia. It was unbelievable! With all the things we've been through, this was the worst of all — it felt like our lives were being crushed. It was so difficult that I didn't know what to do. No experience I've ever been through required so much of me. In fact, I didn't have enough strength to cope with it. Toward the end of this ordeal, I was so weighed down and overwhelmed that I didn't think we'd ever get out! I felt suffocated, trapped, and pinned against the wall. I really thought it was the end of the road for us! As far as we were concerned, the verdict was in, and that verdict said "death." But really, this was no great shock, because we already were feeling the effect of death and depression in our souls.

That is quite a description of a difficult moment in life! But then Paul gloriously added in Second Corinthians 1:10, "Who delivered us from so great a death, and doth deliver: in whom we trust that he will yet deliver us." The Greek phrasing is important because Paul stated, "[God] delivered us." This is past tense. Paul had already experienced deliverance.

"Delivered" is the Greek word *rhuomai*, which means *to deliver from a very deadly or dangerous situation*. Paul said he was delivered from "so great a death...." That phrase "so great" in the Greek is *telikoutos*, and it depicts *something of great magnitude*. Again, "death" is the Greek word *thanatos*, which describes a death verdict which had been issued. Paul said they were delivered from that death sentence. It was a great deliverance.

Then Paul went on to say, "...and doeth deliver...." This is present tense. Right now, God is still delivering us. Finally, Paul concluded that God would "...yet deliver us" — which is future tense in the original Greek. In other words, God *has* delivered us, He *is* delivering us, and He *will* deliver us again in the future. When we factor in the original Greek wording of Second Corinthians 1:10, we get the *Renner Interpretive Version* (*RIV*), which states:

Who has already delivered and rescued us from a serious death sentence, and will deliver and rescue us, and we trust he will keep on delivering and rescuing us.

These are the words of an overcomer! Friend, it doesn't matter what you are facing or what you're going through. Even if you feel exasperated, crushed, or pinned against the wall like there's no way out — *God's delivering power is yours.* Jesus said in John 16:33, "These things I have spoken unto you, that in me ye might have peace. In the world ye shall have tribulation: but be of good cheer; I have overcome the world." You have a victory that overcomes the world. And His overpowering, overcoming promise is yours to claim right now, in Jesus' name. Amen.

STUDY QUESTIONS

Study to shew thyself approved unto God, a workman that needeth
not to be ashamed, rightly dividing the word of truth.
— 2 Timothy 2:15

1. No matter what comes against you, if you'll speak to yourself, cheer yourself up, and grab hold of the power of God, you can overcome anything! Can you recall an instance in the Bible where someone encouraged *himself*? (*Consider* 1 Samuel 30:6.)

2. Throughout the New Testament, Paul didn't hide the fact that he went through hard times. In fact, he spoke about them — particularly in Second Corinthians 1:8-10 — because he wanted to demonstrate that if he could get through what he had been through, *you* can get through what *you're* going through. He made it clear that God had delivered (past tense), does deliver (present tense), and will yet deliver (future tense).

3. You can expect God to deliver you — in the past, the present, and the future! Consider Malachi 3:6, Acts 10:34, and Hebrews 13:8 (*NKJV*). How do these verses reinforce the idea that God is consistent and faithful to deliver His people? Why is it significant that Paul emphasizes God's deliverance in all three tenses (past, present, future) for understanding His character and power?

PRACTICAL APPLICATION

But be ye doers of the word, and not hearers only,
deceiving your own selves.
— James 1:22

1. In John 16:33, Jesus made it clear that in the world we will have tribulation (heavy pressure situations). But He instructs us to "be of good cheer; I have overcome the world." Jesus was so honest with us. The fact is, tight places, heavy burdens, and great squeezes come to all

of us in life. They may be health-related, relational, or financial — and self-inflicted, caused by what somebody else has done, or the result of a demonic attack, but hard times come to us all. If you meditate on the truth that Jesus has overcome the world, it will become easier to do what John 16:33 commands and "be of good cheer." Don't wait for someone to do it for you. Speak to *yourself* and *cheer yourself up*! Use your mouth intentionally to lift your soul out of despair and into faith.

2. To help you be a doer of the Bible truths in this lesson, read First Samuel 30:1-19. Consider how David and his men came to the city and found it was burned, and their wives and children were taken captive. David and those with him wept and were greatly distressed because they were so grieved. But "...David *encouraged himself* in the Lord his God" (1 Samuel 30:6). Next he inquired of the Lord if he should pursue those who created this destruction, and God answered in verse 8, "...Pursue: for thou shalt surely overtake them, and without fail recover all." The awesome news is that according to verse 19, "...David *recovered all*."

The turn in events happened when David encouraged himself in the Lord, then inquired of the Lord amid the tragedy he faced. What about you? If you're in the midst of an intense trial:

-   Encourage yourself in the Lord.

-   Recall past victories.

-   Inquire of the Lord.

-   Obey the Holy Spirit's leading.

-   Experience victory!

LESSON 4

TOPIC

How Did Jesus Describe Overcoming?

SCRIPTURES

1. **Luke 10:17** — And the seventy returned again with joy, saying, Lord, even the devils are subject unto us through thy name.

2. **Luke 10:18** — And he said unto them, I beheld Satan as lightning fall from heaven.

3. **Luke 10:19** — Behold, I give unto you power to tread on serpents and scorpions, and over all the power of the enemy: and nothing shall by any means hurt you.

4. **Luke 10:20** — Notwithstanding in this rejoice not, that the spirits are subject unto you; but rather rejoice, because your names are written in heaven.

5. **Revelation 12:11** — And they overcame him by the blood of the Lamb, and by the word of their testimony.

GREEK WORDS

1. "devils" — **τὰ δαιμόνια** (*ta daimonia*): plural; demons or evil spirits

2. "subject" — **ὑποτάσσω** (*hupotasso*): a military term meaning to subjugate or to dominate; it was used militarily to describe the act of forcing a conquered enemy into a subjugated position

3. "beheld" — **θεάομαι** (*theaomai*): to behold, to see; a spectacle; the Greek root for the word theater

4. "lightning" — **ἀστράπτω** (*astrapto*): a flash of lightning

5. "behold" — **ἰδού** (*idou*): bewilderment, shock, amazement, and wonder

6. "I give" — **δίδωμι** (*didomi*): to give; meaning I hand over, I impart, or I transfer

7. "power" — **ἐξουσία** (*exousia*): authority, influence, or power

8. "tread" — **πατέω** (*pateo*): to tread, to walk, or to walk on a path

9. "on" — **ἐπάνω** (*epano*): above, on, over, or upon; denotes superiority

10. "serpents" — **ὄφις** (*ophis*): plural; serpents or snakes that strike and are often deadly

11. "scorpions" — **σκορπίος** (*skorpios*): plural; scorpions that deliver a sting that can prove debilitating or deadly

12. "over" — **ἐπί** (*epi*): over or upon, denoting a position of superiority

13. "all" — **πᾶσαν** (*pasan*): all; an all-inclusive word that leaves nothing out

14. "power" — **δύναμις** (*dunamis*): power; explosive, superhuman power that comes with enormous energy and produces phenomenal, extraordinary, and unparalleled results

15. "enemy" — ἐχθρός (*echthros*): hate, hatred, hostility; an enemy or opponent; conveys animosity, antagonism, or enmity; describes those who are irreconcilable; used to depict enemies in a military conflict; those engaged in a military conflict; hostile enemies

16. "nothing" — οὐδέν (*ouden*): nothing at all, absolutely nothing; not even one

17. "by any means" — οὐ μὴ (*ou me*): a double negative; no not

18. "hurt" — ἀδικέω (*adikeo*): to suffer injustice or to suffer some kind of wrong or wrongdoing

19. "overcame" — νικάω (*nikao*): one who is overcoming; a champion, victor, or one who possesses some type of superiority; it can be translated to control, to conquer, to defeat, to master, to overcome, to overwhelm, to surpass, or to be victorious; used in Greek literature to portray athletes who had mastered their sport and ultimately reigned supreme as champions in the games; it could also describe a military victory of one foe against the other; it means to be permanently and consistently undeterred in one's efforts to overcome and to obtain a lasting victory

SYNOPSIS

Do you realize the authority Jesus has given to you now that you are born again? In Luke 10:17-20, the disciples of Jesus returned after a time of sharing the Gospel, thrilled that demons had to obey them in Jesus' name. Their celebration was genuine and meaningful, but Jesus redirected their focus. He reminded them of Satan's fall from Heaven, showing that the enemy's defeat was already complete. Then He affirmed their spiritual authority, granting them power to tread on serpents, scorpions, and all the power of the enemy. Yet Jesus emphasized a deeper truth: The greatest reason to rejoice isn't our authority over darkness, but that our names are written in Heaven.

The emphasis of this lesson:

Because of Jesus, you have complete, all-encompassing victory over all the power of the enemy right now, in this world. Yes, rejoice over every triumph you experience, knowing you are an overcomer. But always remember that the greatest triumph you'll ever experience is not victory over your circumstances — it is the promise that your name is written in Heaven, where you will dwell with God forever.

Victory Over the Enemy Brings Joy

Today, we're going to examine what kind of overcoming power Jesus has given to each one of His people. In Luke 10:17-20, we read:

And the seventy returned again with joy, saying, Lord, even the devils are subject unto us through thy name. And he said unto them, I beheld Satan as lightning fall from heaven. Behold, I give unto you power to tread on serpents and scorpions, and over all the power of the enemy: and nothing shall by any means hurt you. Notwithstanding in this rejoice not, that the spirits are subject unto you; but rather rejoice, because your names are written in heaven.

Let's dive into this passage to see all that is contained in these verses, beginning with verse 17: "And the seventy returned again with joy, saying, Lord, even the devils are subject unto us through thy name." When the Bible says these 70 followers of Jesus returned with joy, it carries the idea that they were greatly celebrating and rejoicing. They had just experienced the reality of the power contained in Jesus' name and that with it, they had authority over demon spirits. In the Greek language, the phrase "even the devils" is *ta daimonia*, which is plural. So the disciples of Jesus were declaring that "*a plethora of demons, evil spirits, and devils* are subject unto us through thy name."

The word "subject" is the Greek word *hupotasso*, which is a well-known New Testament word. The word *hupo* means *to be under*, and the word *tasso* means *to order*. When these two Greek words are put together, the resulting term *hupotasso* becomes a military command *to fall in line* or *to obey an order that is given*. It was a military term meaning *to subjugate* or *to dominate*, and it described *the act of forcing a conquered enemy into a subjugated position*.

The 70 were so excited that the Bible says they "returned again with joy." The word "joy" carries the idea that they were jumping up and down. As they were celebrating, they said, in essence, "Lord, Lord, listen to this! Even the devils (plural) — the demons — fall in line and are subject to us. They obey our commands when we use Your name."

In the program, Rick reflected on this verse and his own experience as a young man. He shared:

The first time that I had experience in casting out a demon, it was quite a moment of celebration. I remember it so vividly because I realized that in the name of Jesus, I really have authority over demon spirits. Particularly when I was young, this was new to me, and it was quite a moment of celebration. I don't know if you've ever cast out a demon or if you've ever confronted an evil spirit, but when you do, it is quite a thrill to see how demons submit to you and how they obey your command when you speak to them in the name of Jesus.

Satan Fell Like Lightning

So the 70 disciples returned to Jesus, excited because they had a victorious moment of commanding the evil spirits. These evil spirits fell in line and obeyed them when they used the name of Jesus. Then in Luke 10:18, Jesus replied, "And he said unto them, I beheld Satan as lightning fall from heaven." This was the equivalent of saying, "Hey, guys, let me tell you something. You think you've had quite a moment. I can remember when Satan was cast out of Heaven. I beheld it."

The Greek word for "beheld" is *theaomai*. It's connected to the word *theatron*, which is where we get the word for a *theater*. It means *to watch something from the beginning to the end*, just like watching a theatrical performance from the beginning of Act One all the way to the end of the last act.

Jesus saw the whole thing, and it was quite a spectacle. He said, "...I beheld Satan as lightning fall from heaven" (Luke 10:18). In Greek, the phrase "as lightning" describes *a flash of lightning*. Jesus was telling us how fast Satan fell when he was expelled from Heaven.

The devil is a defeated foe. Jesus was there when he was cast out, and He told the 70, in essence, "Hey, guys, I'm glad that you experienced a moment of jubilation, but let me tell you, I can remember when this defeated foe was cast out of Heaven. Boom! He was gone like a flash of light."

Jesus' Power Is Given to Us

Jesus continues in Luke 10:19, "Behold, I give unto you power to tread on serpents and scorpions, and over all the power of the enemy: and nothing shall by any means hurt you." The word "behold" in this verse is translated from the Greek word *idou*, which is used repeatedly in the New Testament and always carries the idea of *bewilderment, shock, amazement, and wonder.* In this particular verse, Jesus inserted the word, *idou*, to express His own sense of amazement at what He was about to tell the 70. It is the equivalent of saying, "Wow, listen to this. This is absolutely amazing."

Jesus was excited about what He was about to say to His followers. And friend, you ought to be excited to hear it! Jesus said, "Behold! Wow, this is amazing. Listen to this. Hold onto your seat." Then He added, "I give unto you power."

The phrase "I give" is translated from a form of the Greek word *didomi* — meaning *to give, to hand over, to impart,* or *to transfer.* Jesus literally said in this verse, "I'm going to give, hand over, impart, transfer, and transmit to you — right now — power." Here, "power" is a form of the Greek word *exousia,* which is the word for *authority.* It carries the idea of *influence and power.* This is not just power — this is *authority that is influential.* It is *influential power.* Jesus said, "I'm going to give you power so great that it will give you the ability to influence the whole spiritual realm."

'Power To Tread'

What does this authority mean to us? In Luke 10:19, Jesus instructs us specifically to "tread on serpents and scorpions…." In the original Greek, "tread" comes from the word *pateo,* meaning *to tread, to walk,* or *to walk on a path.* Now this idea is very important. We are exhorted by the Lord to walk on a path and "on serpents and scorpions."

The word "on" is the Greek term *epano,* which means *above, on, over,* or *upon.* It denotes *superiority.* In the Greek text, "serpents" is plural and refers to *serpents or snakes that strike in order to kill.* "Scorpions" is the Greek word *skorpios.* It is also plural, and it describes *scorpions that could deliver a deadly sting.* Jesus was declaring to us, "I give you authority, influential authority, to tread, to walk on, to walk right on top of, to walk upon serpents and scorpions."

This promise was important because Jesus was going to send His disciples to the ends of the earth to preach the Gospel. In the First Century, there were not always roads to go where the disciples needed to go. Any roads that did exist often had ruts in which snakes would lie. If there were no snakes, there would be scorpions. People who traveled always faced the prospect of having to deal with serpents and scorpions, and this was a big terror to travelers.

The 70 had just returned and were so excited because they found out that even demons were subject to them in the name of Jesus. Then Jesus declares to them, "Behold! Listen to this. Hold onto your seat. This is exciting! As I send you forth and you begin to travel on paths, I'm even going to give you the ability to walk right over and tread on serpents and scorpions."

We have the promise of Jesus that when we travel, we have the authority to go forth in His name without fear of anything disrupting our travel or harming us. Today, we don't worry about serpents and scorpions, but when we get on a plane, we can lay our hand on that plane before we walk into the aircraft and speak this promise of God over it. Jesus has given us authority to go, and if we go in His name, we have authority to tread on anything the devil tries to put in our way. We have a position of superiority.

You Have Authority Over Anything the Enemy Attempts

Next, Jesus went on to declare that we have power not only over serpents and scorpions, but also "over all the power of the enemy...." In other words, He broadens His promise. In the Greek, the word "over" is *epi*, which means *over or upon, denoting a position of superiority.* Twice in Luke 10:17-20, we find that Jesus has given His people *a position of superiority* over all the power of the enemy.

The word "all" is the Greek word *pasan*, an *all-inclusive* term that conveys the idea of *absolutely everything.* It *leaves nothing out.* "Power" is the Greek word *dunamis*, which describes *superhuman power that comes with enormous energy and produces phenomenal, extraordinary, amazing, and unparalleled results.* This tells us the devil does sometimes exhibit real power. But we have a superior position over all the power of the enemy!

Notice that Jesus refers to the devil as "the enemy." In the original Greek, "enemy" is *echthros*, a term that literally denotes *an enemy or opponent* and conveys the idea of *animosity, antagonism, or enmity.* It describes *those who are irreconcilable* and is used to depict *enemies in a military conflict* or *hostile enemies.*

Friend, the devil is not someone we can get along with. He is *hostile* toward us. It is impossible to be reconciled with the enemy. He wants to get in our way, stop us, and do everything he can to thwart us. He desires to strike us, sting us, and stop us along the way.

But Jesus said, in effect, "Behold! Wow, listen to this! I'm handing over, giving, imparting, and transferring to *you* influential authority and power so great that it will give you the ability to tread right on top of serpents. It doesn't matter how many the devil sends your way. You have the ability to tread on all these serpents and scorpions — anything that comes in life to sting you and to immobilize, you have the power to keep walking right over them."

Rejoice That Your Name Is Written in Heaven

Rick shared that whenever the devil tries to get in his way or in the way of RENNER Ministries, he always says, "Devil, you might as well move because *we're not stopping.* We have the authority to keep walking. If you stand in front of us, we're going to knock you flat because Jesus has given us the ability to trample on top of *you* and not just on top of these serpents and scorpions that you've tried to use to derail us."

The phrase "over all" in Luke 10:19 means *absolutely all* — it is *all-inclusive* and *leaves nothing out.* This is the kind of authority we have over all the power of the enemy. The devil is a hostile enemy, but we have influential authority over him. We have an overcoming power.

Next Jesus went on to declare in verse 19, "…And nothing shall by any means hurt you." That is quite a promise! The word "nothing" in the original Greek is *ouden,* which means *nothing at all, absolutely nothing.* Literally, it means *not even one.* Not even one thing shall hurt you.

The phrase "by any means" in Greek is *ou me.* It is a double negative, meaning *no not,* a phrase that is not necessary unless one is trying to make a very strong point. Jesus was saying that these things shall not hurt you. The word "hurt" is the Greek word *adikeo,* which means *to suffer an injustice* or *to suffer some kind of wrong or a wrongdoing.*

In the original Greek language, there are *three negatives* in this verse. It could literally be translated, "and nothing, indeed not, absolutely nothing, by no means shall hurt you." Jesus used three negatives in the Greek language to tell us what kind of authority He has given to us. It is *overcoming authority — and nothing, indeed not, absolutely nothing, by no means will hurt us.* You must embrace that verse and take it by faith.

Jesus concluded in Luke 10:20 with a message of powerful wisdom: "Notwithstanding in this rejoice not, that the spirits are subject unto you; but rather rejoice, because your names are written in heaven." In other words, the very fact that demons listen to you and fall in line when you speak is evidence that you are a real child of God. And while it is exciting to see demon spirits fall in line, the most exciting part is that it is evidence that you are an authentic child of God. And that is why these evil spirits are obeying you.

You Are Destined To Overcome

Let's end our study with one final verse that talks about the overcoming ability Jesus has given to us. Revelation 12:11 says, "And they overcame him by the blood of the Lamb, and by the word of their testimony...." Here again we see the word "overcame," which is the same Greek word *nikao* that we have examined in previous lessons. It describes *one who is overcoming.* It depicts *a champion, a victor,* or *one who possesses some type of superiority* and can be translated *to control, to conquer, to defeat, to master, to overcome, to overwhelm, to surpass,* or *to be victorious.*

The Greek word *nikao* was used in Greek literature to portray *athletes who mastered their sport and ultimately reigned as supreme champions in the games.* It could be used in military contexts to describe *a victory of one foe against the other.* And it meant *to be permanently and consistently undeterred in one's efforts to overcome and to obtain a lasting victory.* All of this rich meaning is contained in this word "overcame" in Revelation 12:11 — "And they overcame him by the blood of the Lamb, and by the word of their testimony...."

God has called you to be an overcomer. We've seen it again and again and again in the Scriptures. Jesus has given you influential authority over serpents, over scorpions, and over all the work of the enemy. You have everything you need to push the enemy out of the way, trample on top of him, keep moving forward, and guarantee that nothing shall by any means hurt you. Take it by faith and know that Jesus has given you power to overcome the enemy.

STUDY QUESTIONS

Study to shew thyself approved unto God, a workman that needeth
not to be ashamed, rightly dividing the word of truth.
— 2 Timothy 2:15

1. As the disciples were celebrating that demons were subject to them in Jesus' name, in Luke 10:20, Jesus redirected their excitement by pointing to an even more profound blessing — their salvation! The authority Jesus gave us over the enemy is a great help in this world, but having your name written in Heaven is an eternal, unlimited blessing! How can you be sure you're going to Heaven when you die? (*Consider* John 3:16-17; Acts 2:21; and Romans 10:9,13.)

2. In Luke 10:18, Jesus declared, "...I beheld Satan *as lightning* fall from heaven." When did Jesus behold this event? What caused Satan to fall from Heaven? (*Consider* Isaiah 14:12-15 and Ezekiel 28:12-18.)

3. Jesus gave us power (authority) "to tread on serpents and scorpions, and over *all* the power of the enemy: and *nothing* shall *by any means* hurt you" (Luke 10:19). What all-inclusive terms did Jesus use in this verse? Is there anything the devil can throw at you that you *don't* have authority over? What else does the Bible tell us about our authority over the enemy? (*Consider* Psalm 91:13; Mark 16:18; and Acts 28:5.)

PRACTICAL APPLICATION

But be ye doers of the word, and not hearers only,
deceiving your own selves.
— James 1:22

1. There's no need to be afraid of the enemy or the attacks he launches against you, your family, and the plan of God for your life. God gave you authority over *all* the power of the enemy. Keep moving forward by faith and tread on the evil one's attacks against you in the name of Jesus! Don't allow sickness, disease, delay, or distraction to deter your progress on your God-given path. Arise, take your authority, and advance in the call of God on your life today, in Jesus' name! How can you "tread on" the enemy's schemes this week by faith, even in situations that seem overwhelming or discouraging?

2. You have everything you need to push the enemy out of the way, trample on top of him, keep moving forward, and guarantee that

nothing shall by any means hurt you. Take it by faith and know that Jesus has given you power to overcome the enemy. Write Luke 10:19 down and put it in a place you can see it daily as a reminder to *exercise* your authority and keep moving forward!

3. The most significant triumph you'll ever experience is not victory over your circumstances — it is the promise that your name is written in Heaven, where you will live in the presence of God for eternity! Take a moment now to pray these powerful verses: "Restore unto me the joy of thy salvation; and uphold me with thy free spirit. Then will I teach transgressors thy ways; and sinners shall be converted unto thee" (Psalm 51:12-13). If you are born again, your name is written in Heaven. Allow God to restore the joy of your salvation, and you will find yourself teaching others about Him and leading others *to Jesus*.

Psalm 51:12-13 speaks of the joy of salvation and leading others to God. In what ways can restoring or embracing that joy affect how you influence or teach others about Him?

LESSON 5

TOPIC
Can You Access Overcoming Power?

SCRIPTURES

1. **Ephesians 6:10** — Finally, my brethren, be strong in the Lord, and in the power of his might.

2. **Ephesians 6:11** — Put on the whole armour of God, that ye may be able to stand against the wiles of the devil.

3. **Ephesians 6:13** — Wherefore take unto you the whole armour of God....

GREEK WORDS

1. "strong" — ἐνδυναμόω (*endunamoo*): to render strong; to be inwardly strengthened; a compound of ἐν (*en*), which means in, and δύναμις (*dunamis*), which normally indicates phenomenal power and strength; explosive, unparalleled power

2. "power" — **κράτος** (*kratos*): force, strength, or might; manifested power; demonstrated, eruptive power

3. "might" — **ἰσχύς** (*ischus*): ability, force, or strength; the strength of God bestowed upon believers; describes a mighty individual, a mighty man, or a man who is muscle-bound

4. "put on" — **ἐνδύω** (*enduo*): to enter into; to get into, as into clothes; to put on; to be endued

5. "take unto you" — **ἀναλαμβάνω** (*analambano*): a compound of **ἀνα** (*ana*), meaning to repeat or to do what you used to do, and **λαμβάνω** (*lambano*), which means to take; as a compound, it means to take unto you; to take to oneself; to receive

SYNOPSIS

When you were born again, you were placed in Christ — which is where the phenomenal, unparalleled power of God to defeat the enemy also dwells. This power is at hand whenever you need it. In Ephesians 6, the apostle Paul urged believers to "be strong in the Lord" (v. 10), drawing their strength from His mighty power that overcomes every obstacle. This is made possible because we are *in Christ*, fully armed and ready to experience victory.

The emphasis of this lesson:

You are literally a container of God's power! You are already positioned perfectly *in Christ*, surrounded by His supernatural strength every moment. As you continually choose to receive fresh infillings from Him, you are empowered day by day to go forth and be victorious over all the power of the enemy.

A Final Word To Lead Us Forward

As we conclude our study on the overcoming power we have in Christ, let's examine Ephesians 6. In the book of Ephesians, the apostle Paul was writing to the Ephesian church, covering many important things. In chapter one, he covered election, predestination, and the fact that we've been chosen and sealed by the Holy Spirit — an important truth!

In chapter two, Paul talked about the grace of God and the fact that we've been quickened together with Christ. He discussed the eternal plan of God in the Church in chapter three. Then in chapter four, he shared on the unity of the faith, the five-fold ministry, and all kinds of wonderful things. He exhorted the Ephesians in chapter five about the relationship between husbands and wives and between employers and employees, and at the start of chapter six, he covered the relationship between parents and children. There is so much in the book of Ephesians!

Finally, we get to Ephesians 6:10, which says, "Finally, my brethren, be strong in the Lord, and in the power of his might." The word "finally" carries the idea that Paul was moving on to the last and most important point. It was like saying, "I have saved the most important thing to the end. If you can't remember anything else I've said, please remember this." Paul began to give us the final and most important word.

Remember, Paul covered a lot of important things in this epistle. But now he declared, "Let me tell you what is most important for you to recall." Often, when you write a letter, you save the most important thing to the very end because when people are finished reading, you want that to stay in their minds. That's what he did.

You Are Strong in Christ

In Ephesians 6:10, Paul wrote, "Finally, my brethren, be strong in the Lord, and in the power of his might." The word "strong" is a form of the Greek word *endunamoo*, a compound of the word *en*, which means *to be in, as though to put something in a vessel or receptacle*, and the word *dunamoo*, a form of the Greek word *dunamis*, which describes *explosive, unparalleled power*. When you put the two words together, it depicts *a power that is designed to be placed into a vessel or some kind of receptacle*. We are the vessels! We are the receptacles.

God has designed us to contain His supernatural *dunamis*. His *phenomenal, unparalleled power* has been designed to fit in us — it is not just free-floating in the universe. God designed His Holy Ghost power to be *placed in us*. We are to be the containers of His power.

Notice the verse says, "Be strong in the Lord...." In the Greek text, this is the locative case. It means being locked up in the person of Christ. The *only* place you will find this power is in the person of Christ. This power is *in* Christ. Well, according to Ephesians 2:10, *you are in Christ*.

You are locked up in the person of Jesus Christ. And because we are in Christ, God "hath blessed us with all spiritual blessings in heavenly places in Christ" (Ephesians 1:3). According to Ephesians 6:10, we also have access to this amazing *dunamis* power, which is also locked up in the person of Jesus Christ. You are constantly rubbing elbows with this power because you are in Him. This supernatural, phenomenal power is contained inside the person of Christ. All you have to do is reach out in faith and embrace it. Just say, "Lord, I'm accepting Your power."

On the program, Rick recalled that early in their ministry, he and Denise were ministering in a large Pentecostal denominational church. At the end of the service, he invited people to come forward who had never been filled with the Holy Spirit. He shared:

> I was shocked at the response because the altar was filled from one side all the way to the other end with people who had never been filled with the Holy Spirit. I was stunned by that. I went down to the front and began to lay hands on them to pray for them to receive the baptism in the Holy Spirit. The pastor followed me and said, 'Son, I'll take it from here.' I listened as he said to each one of them, 'Pray harder. You've got to tarry. You've got to plead.' He made it such a work of the flesh. Some of those people had been tarrying and waiting more than 40 years to be filled with the Holy Spirit.

Friend, it's not hard to receive the baptism in the Holy Spirit. You are in Christ, and according to Ephesians 6:10, you have access to the power of God that is locked up in the person of Christ. You are surrounded by this divine power. You're rubbing elbows with it! You and the power of God are both in the person of Jesus, which means all you have to do is reach out and accept it by faith. God has made it easy. Rick went on to share:

> I'm thinking about moments in my own life when Denise and I are traveling. We're trying to get to a meeting. Our flight has been delayed, so we get there late. We rush to the meeting, huffing and puffing. I really don't have time to prepare myself. Often I think, *How am I going to be able to minister in this condition?*
>
> So I go off to a place by myself and I always say, 'All right, Lord, I'm in Christ. The power's in Christ. I'm late for the meeting. I don't have time to tarry. So Lord, I'm just taking Your power. Fill me right now.' And every time, I receive a fresh infilling of the Holy Spirit. My friends, it is yours for the taking!

The truth is simple but profound: You don't have to earn this power, struggle to conjure it, or wait decades to experience it. You are already in Christ, and the same supernatural power that raised Christ from the grave is available to you right now. All that is required is faith. Reach out, believe, and receive it. Step into the fullness of your inheritance, knowing that the power of God is not only accessible but ready to move in you the moment you open your heart and say, "Lord, I receive your power."

Be Refilled With God's Power Again and Again!

Now there's the initial baptism in the Holy Spirit, but after that, there are many, many infillings. For example, in Acts 2, all the people who were in the Upper Room were baptized in the Holy Spirit. But did you know that by the time you get to Acts 4, they received a fresh infilling? When you get to Acts 5, there was another fresh infilling. There's one initial experience where you're baptized in the Holy Spirit, but after that, there are many, many moments when you receive new infillings. Rick shared that part of his daily routine is to read the Bible early in the morning and then ask the Holy Spirit to refill him. We don't have to plead or beg for it to happen. We just need to open our hearts and embrace that we are in Christ.

The power of God is in Christ, and God wants to fill and refill us. This power is ours for the taking. The apostle Paul declared, "Finally, my brethren, be strong in the Lord…" (Ephesians 6:10). In other words, "If you don't remember anything else, please remember this. God has created His power to be placed inside you. My friends, be filled with this divine power in the Lord."

The rest of this verse declares we are to do this "…in the power of his might." The word "power" is the Greek word *kratos*, which is used in Scripture to describe *force, strength, might, and manifested power*. It is *demonstrated, eruptive power*. It's not just theoretical power that you hear about. You can *see* this power. You can *feel* it. For example, when Jesus was raised from the dead, the word *kratos* is used to depict the power that raised Him from the dead. The soldiers who were guarding the tomb didn't just theoretically believe in the power. They felt the power. It was *eruptive* — it was *demonstrated*.

When we receive a fresh infilling of the Holy Spirit, the power of the Holy Spirit comes into us. This power comes not just to reside in us, but to manifest. It wants to demonstrate. It wants to erupt in signs, wonders, and mighty deeds. God wants to heal people through your hands. He wants demons to be cast out with your authoritative voice. Signs and wonders are to follow you everywhere you go. When this power comes in, it immediately wants to manifest in an eruptive, demonstrated way.

God's Power Is Mighty To Deliver

Ephesians 6:10 goes on to say, "…and in the power of his might." In the Greek text, the word "might" is *ischus*. Usually in the King James Version, *ischus* is translated as "might," but it describes *a mighty individual, a mighty man*, or *a man who is muscle-bound*. If you've ever seen people who give themselves to bodybuilding, they're strapping with muscles. Their muscles are enormous. When they flex their arms, the size of their muscles is just amazing.

This word "might" in the original Greek describes *a mighty man* or *a man who is muscle-bound*. But notice that this verse instructs, "Be strong in the Lord, and in the power of his might." It's talking about *God's* might. The apostle Paul was depicting God as a mighty man, a man bound with muscles.

If you could see the right arm of God, what kind of arm would He have? He would truly be Mr. Universe. There is no one in the universe to compare with the muscular, mighty ability of God. Think about it! He just flexed His muscle and destroyed the Egyptian empire (*see* Exodus 14:27-28). He flexed His muscle, and the Red Sea was parted (*see* Exodus 14:21). He flexed His muscle, and Jesus was raised from the dead (*see* Ephesians 1:19-20).

When the power of the Holy Spirit comes into us, it is such an overcoming, conquering power because it connects us to the muscular abilities of God. This is why we need to be filled with the Holy Spirit. Without His power, we are weaklings. Even though we're saved, we're puny. But when we receive the empowerment of the Holy Spirit, it divinely connects us to the muscular ability of God.

As mere human beings, when we pray in the name of Jesus, God flexes His muscle, and His power flows in us and through us. That power is eruptive, and it is demonstrative. We can see the power right in front of us. We can drive back hell because of this power Ephesians is describing.

You Can Access Overcoming Power by Being Filled With the Holy Spirit

Ephesians 6:11 says, "Put on the whole armour of God, that ye may be able to stand against the wiles of the devil." The phrase "put on" is the Greek word *enduo* — and it tells us *how* we put on the whole armor of God. Some people get up every morning and go through gyrations where they say, "I'm going to put on my breastplate of righteousness. Now, I'm going to put on my helmet of salvation. And now I'll put on my loin belt of truth." But that is just a mental exercise.

According to this verse, what puts the whole armor on you is when you've received an endowment of power. "Put on" is the same word *enduo* that is translated as "strong" in verse 10. It means that when you are endued with power — when the power of God hits you — *it is His power* that puts the helmet of salvation on you.

The power of God puts the breastplate of righteousness and the loin belt of truth on you. His power gives you the shield of faith and greaves and shoes of peace. It puts a sword in your hand. It is the power of God that totally outfits you. And as long as you're walking in *His* power, you are totally outfitted with all the weaponry you need to put the devil on the run. But the moment you walk away from the power of God, the weaponry begins to fall off you.

That's what happened to the Ephesians. We see this in Ephesians 6:13, where Paul instructed, "Wherefore take unto you the whole armour of God...." The phrase "take unto you" is the Greek word *analambano*, a compound of the word *ana*, meaning *to repeat* or *to do what you used to do*, and the word *lambano*, meaning *to take*. Put together, these words form a compound that means *to take unto you, to do it like you used to do*, and *to reach down and pick up* the armor. This means the Ephesians were not wearing the armor of God. The armor was lying around their feet.

So Paul exhorted them, saying in effect, "Hey! Based on the instruction that I've just given you, I'm telling you how to put the armor of God back on. Reach down, pick it up, and put it back on." You don't put on the armor by just mentally going through an exercise: "Now I'm going to pick up my shield of faith." According to verses 10-11, it is that endowment of power that puts the helmet and weaponry on you. When the power of

God hits you, not only does it fill you — it begins to dress you with all the weaponry you need to put the enemy on the run. It is amazing!

Do you see why it's not optional for you to be baptized in the Holy Spirit and not receive a refill? The only way you will consistently walk in the power of God and the weaponry of God is if you are consistently filled and refilled. As long as the power of God is filling you, you'll be dressed in spiritual weaponry and have within you the power that conquers and overcomes. You'll have the ability to drive back the forces of hell itself. Wow!

Receive a Fresh Infilling of God's Power Right Now!

Now let's look again at Ephesians 6:10, where Paul was saying, in essence, "Finally, to the last and most important point! Hey, if you can't remember anything else, don't forget this. My brethren, be strong — *enduo*. Receive an endowment of divine power." The word *en* means *inside, like the place in a receptacle or in a container*. The word *duo* comes from *dunamis* and depicts *explosive, unparalleled power*. Paul was declaring that God has fashioned you to hold the power he was talking about, and it's in the Lord. This power is not somewhere out there. It's *in Christ*. That's the only place you'll find this power.

The greatest aspect of this? If you are born again, *you* are in Christ! You are locked up in the person of Jesus, which means God has made this so simple. You don't have to beat yourself up. You don't have to beg, plead, or tarry. All you need to do is say, "Hey, Lord, I'm in need of fresh infilling. I'm dealing with some rough stuff, and I need to know that I'm walking in divine weaponry. I need power in me to push back the forces of hell."

When we ask this, Jesus responds. He says, in essence, "All right, open your heart. Open your arms and receive." It's that easy. God has made it that easy because He knew we couldn't do it if it were complicated. All you have to do right now is say, "Lord, I take Your power. Fill me. Fill me anew."

If you've never been baptized in the Holy Spirit, say right now, "Jesus, baptize me in the Holy Spirit." Friend, He will fill you with divine power. You're made for it. That power will begin to operate mightily through you. It will connect you to God's mighty, muscular ability, and it will dress you with the spiritual weaponry you need to put the enemy on the run.

STUDY QUESTIONS

Study to shew thyself approved unto God, a workman that needeth
not to be ashamed, rightly dividing the word of truth.
— 2 Timothy 2:15

1. You can access overcoming power by being filled with the Holy Spirit,
   which is a special and empowering gift. Every born-again believer can
   receive the baptism in the Holy Spirit. What does the Bible teach us
   about *receiving* the baptism in the Holy Spirit? (*Consider* Luke 11:13;
   Acts 1:8, 2:4, 10:45-46, and 19:6.)

2. There is one initial baptism in the Holy Spirit, but after that, there can
   be many refillings. For example, in Acts 2:4, all the people who were in
   the Upper Room were baptized in the Holy Spirit. Then in Acts 4:31,
   they received a fresh infilling. What does Ephesians 5:18-19 tell us
   about being filled with the Spirit?

3. When you receive a fresh infilling of the Holy Spirit, the power of God
   comes into you, and the Holy Spirit immediately wants to manifest
   and demonstrate. How does Second Corinthians 2:14 illustrate the
   way God works through believers to triumph over spiritual opposition?
   (*Consider* Matthew 28:18-19; Mark 16:15-18; and Acts 4:29-30.)

PRACTICAL APPLICATION

But be ye doers of the word, and not hearers only,
deceiving your own selves.
— James 1:22

1. Are you in need of a fresh infilling of the Holy Spirit? The good news
   is that you don't have to beg, plead, or tarry to receive. Take time today
   to ask God in faith for that guaranteed fresh infilling! All you need
   to do is say, *Lord, I'm in need of fresh infilling. I'm dealing with some
   challenging things. Right now, I receive a fresh infilling of the Holy Spirit.
   Thank You, Father, in Jesus' name. Amen.*

2. Review the main point of each lesson and arm yourself with the truth
   of God's Word. John 16:33 declares, "…In the world ye shall have
   tribulation: but be of good cheer; I have overcome the world." Jesus
   overcame the world, and He lives inside you — so cheer up! You're an
   overcomer!

   • Victory is yours to claim!

- Jesus triumphed over hell.
- *You* can overcome the world.
- Rejoice! Your name is written in Heaven!
- Be continually filled with the Holy Spirit.

3. The only way you will consistently walk in the power of God and the weaponry of God is if you are being consistently filled and refilled with the Holy Spirit. As long as the power of God is filling you, you'll be dressed in spiritual weaponry and have within you power that conquers and overcomes. You'll have the ability to drive back the forces of hell itself. You are an overcomer! Write down the most important insights you received from these lessons, ask the Holy Spirit to help you consistently be a "doer" of them, and share them with someone who needs them.

A Prayer To Receive Salvation

If you've never received Jesus as your Savior and Lord, now is the time for you to experience the new life Jesus wants to give you! To receive God's gift of salvation that can be obtained through Jesus alone, pray this prayer from your heart:

Jesus, I repent of my sin and receive You as my Savior and Lord. Wash away my sin with Your precious blood and make me completely new. I thank You that my sin is removed, and Satan no longer has any right to lay claim on me. Through Your empowering grace, I faithfully promise that I will serve You as my Lord for the rest of my life.

If you just prayed this prayer of salvation, you are born again! You are a brand-new creation in Christ! Would you please let us know of your decision by going to **renner.org/salvation**? We would love to connect with you and pray for you as you begin your new life in Christ.

Scriptures for further study: John 3:16; John 14:6; Acts 4:12; Ephesians 1:7; Hebrews 10:19,20; 1 Peter 1:18,19; Romans 10:9,10; Colossians 1:13; 2 Corinthians 5:17; Romans 6:4; 1 Peter 1:3

CLAIM YOUR FREE RESOURCE!

As a way of introducing you further to the teaching ministry of Rick Renner, we would like to send you FREE of charge his teaching, "How To Receive a Miraculous Touch From God" on CD or as an MP3 download.

In His earthly ministry, Jesus commonly healed *all* who were sick of *all* their diseases. In this profound message, learn about the manifold dimensions of Christ's wisdom, goodness, power, and love toward all humanity who came to Him in faith with their needs.

☑ **YES, I want to receive Rick Renner's monthly teaching letter!**

Simply scan the QR code to claim this resource or go to: **renner.org/claim-your-free-offer**

Connect WITH US!

R renner.org

f facebook.com/rickrenner • facebook.com/rennerdenise

▶ youtube.com/rennerministries • youtube.com/deniserenner

◉ instagram.com/rickrrenner • instagram.com/rennerministries_
instagram.com/rennerdenise

Dear Friend,

If you enjoyed this study guide and believe others would benefit from reading it, please leave a review on Amazon and recommend it to others — or *consider sharing a copy with a friend or loved one!*

There is a great need for *"teaching you can trust"* among God's people.

Your friends in Christ and for His Gospel,

Dirk & Denise Renner

www.ingramcontent.com/pod-product-compliance
Lightning Source LLC
Chambersburg PA
CBHW071645040426
42452CB00009B/1765